COUNTRIES IN OUR WORLD

SPAIN
IN OUR WORLD

Sean Ryan

Published by Smart Apple Media
P.O. Box 3263, Mankato, Minnesota 56002

Printed in the United States of America at Corporate
Graphics, in North Mankato, Minnesota.

Published by arrangement with the Watts Publishing
Group Ltd., London.

Library of Congress Cataloging-in-Publication Data

Ryan, Sean, 1957-
  Spain in our world / by Sean Ryan.
     p. cm. -- (Countries in our world)
  Summary: "Describes the economy, government, and
culture of Spain today and discusses Spain's influence
of and relations with the rest of the world"--Provided
by publisher.
  Includes index.
  ISBN 978-1-59920-438-3 (library binding)
  1. Spain--Juvenile literature. I. Title.
  DP17.R93 2011
  946.083--dc22
                                          2009043164

Produced by: White-Thomson Publishing Ltd.

Series consultant: Rob Bowden
Editor: Sonya Newland
Designer: Alix Wood
Picture researcher: Amy Sparks

Picture Credits
Corbis: Cover (David Samuel Robbins), 9 (O.
Alamany & E. Vicens), 14 (Chris Sattleberger),
15 (Paul Hanna/Reuters), 18 (Daiju Kitamura/AFLO
SPORT/Icon SMI), 20 (Charles O'Rear), 21 (Albert
Gea/Reuters), 24 (Manual H. de Leon/epa), 26
(Laurent Dard/Reuters); **Dreamstime:** 4 (Joe Stark),
7 (Faberfoto), 8 (Haak78), 12 (Jarnogz), 25 (Gvictoria),
29 (Jarnogz); **iStock:** 10 (Elena Aliaga), 28 (Graham
Heywood); **Fotolia:** 11 (Marta P), 22 (Freefly);
Photoshot: 27 (EFE/UPPA); **Shutterstock:** 1 (Regien
Paassen), 6 (PixAchi), 17 (Geanina Bechea), 23
(Regien Paassen); **Simon Rice:** 13, 16, 19.

1207
32010

9 8 7 6 5 4 3 2 1

Contents

Introducing Spain

Spain is situated on the Iberian Peninsula, at the far western end of Europe. In the last 50 years, Spain has changed from being one of the most isolated countries in the Western world to having global connections. It is now an important and influential country as part of the European Union (EU). Spanish is also the third most common language in the world, after Mandarin Chinese and English.

▲ *Spain shares borders with France, Portugal, Andorra, and Gibraltar—a British territory.*

The Heart of Spain

Spain is divided into several regions, each with different landscapes and peoples. Castile, in the middle of the country, is centered around the capital, Madrid, and has a harsh landscape of broad plains and rugged mountains. The name Castile means "Land of Castles," and there are many forts on the hilltops of Castile. The people who live there—Castilians—have been the dominant force in Spain since the fifteenth century. They sponsored the first voyages of discovery to the Americas and established colonies there, making Spain the world's first major colonial power.

IT'S A FACT!

When it was built during the eighth century, the mosque at Cordoba was the second largest in the world, and it was one of the most important places in the Islamic Empire. The Moorish influence can be seen in its architecture.

▶ *The inside of the mosque at Cordoba has more than 1,000 pillars supporting arches designed in the Moorish style. It became a Roman Catholic cathedral in A.D. 1236.*

Moorish Influences

Castile was formed in the eighth century, when a number of smaller kingdoms joined together to fight a group of Islamic peoples from North Africa called the Moors, who were invading the Iberian Peninsula. The Moors conquered much of Spain, and the area they ruled was called Al-Andaluz. The modern region Andalusia covers most of southern Spain and the Moorish influence is still strong there—it can be seen in the architecture and food, for example. This is the most populated of Spain's regions, and the people who live here are called Andalusians.

The Mediterranean

Along the coast of the Mediterranean Sea—Spain's top tourist destination—is a region called Catalonia. The Catalans were a great seafaring and trading nation long before the Castilians set off to explore foreign lands. Influences from the time when Spain was part of the Roman Empire can still be seen in Catalonia, particularly in the language, Catalan, which is closely related to Latin. The capital, Barcelona, is considered one of the world's greatest cultural centers today.

▲ *The Guggenheim Museum is one of the most famous landmarks in Bilbao,*
in the Basque Country. It houses work by Spanish and international artists.

An Inward View

The Basque Country crosses the border into
France. Cut off by mountains and the sea,
the Basques are an ancient people who speak
Euskara, a language that is not related to
any other. Many of the world's pioneering
navigators were Basque people, and Basque
vessels were renowned for being the best in
the world. The Basques adapted this heritage
during the Industrial Revolution, and today
the region is still Spain's industrial heartland,
based around the great port city of Bilbao.

The Far West

The far western region of Galicia, jutting into
the Atlantic Ocean, has been isolated from
the rest of the country for much of Spain's
history. The people who live there have Celtic
origins, and still have much in common with
the Irish and the Scots. Galicia has its own
language, Gallego, which is a Romance
language of Latin origin, like Spanish and
Catalan. Galicia has been nicknamed "the
land of a thousand rivers," because so many
rivers and streams run through it.

BASIC DATA

Official Name: Kingdom of Spain

Capital: Madrid

Size: 194,897 sq miles (504,782 sq km)

Population: 40,525,002 (2009 est).

Currency: Euro

Spain Today

Throughout history, Spain's fortunes have risen and fallen. It has conquered many areas but has also been torn apart by civil wars. It has been one of the world's greatest powers and one of Europe's poorest countries. Rivalries between the different regions affect its politics, and its varied geography plays an important part in the economy. But Spain's ties to the Mediterranean and Islamic worlds, and the legacy of its empire in Latin America, make it a unique "bridge" between these regions and its place in Europe.

FAMOUS SPANIARD

Francisco Franco (1892–1975)

Francisco Franco ruled Spain from the end of the Spanish Civil War in 1939 until 1975. He was the only fascist dictator to remain in power after World War II (1939-45). It is believed that more than 130,000 people were murdered on Franco's orders during this time.

▼ *People enjoy boating in a park in Madrid, which became Spain's capital in 1561.*

Landscapes and Environment

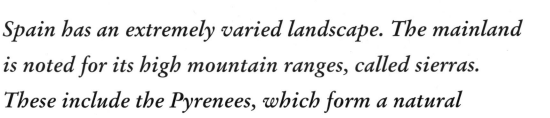

Spain has an extremely varied landscape. The mainland is noted for its high mountain ranges, called sierras. These include the Pyrenees, which form a natural boundary between Spain and its neighbor, France. The Balearic Islands in the Mediterranean Sea and the sub-tropical Canary Islands in the Atlantic Ocean, off the coast of North Africa, add to the diversity of Spain's landscapes and environments.

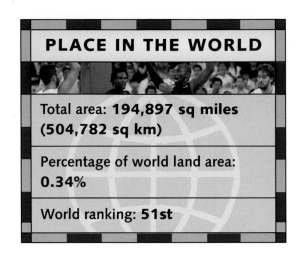

PLACE IN THE WORLD

Total area: **194,897 sq miles (504,782 sq km)**

Percentage of world land area: **0.34%**

World ranking: **51st**

Warm Weather

The rugged north coast of Spain faces the stormy Atlantic Ocean. A high mountain range, called the Cordillera Cantabrica, closely follows the coast, where warm, moist air produces a lot of rainfall. The coastline along the southeast of the country has its own Mediterranean climate, with hot summers and mild winters. However, most of the mainland is a high, dry plateau called the Meseta Central. This has a continental climate, with severe cold in winter and extreme heat in summer.

▼ *Spain's highest mountain, El Teide on the Canary Island of Tenerife, is a dormant volcano in one of the country's 14 national parks.*

Europe's Last Wilderness

Much of the Meseta is dry scrubland called *dehesa*. There are some desert areas, but this huge region is divided by the sierras. The high mountain peaks cause rainfall that feeds the rivers, including Spain's largest river, the Ebro. The mountains and river valleys provide shelter for dense forests to grow—nearly 30 percent of Spain is covered in forest, more compared to the country's land area than many other European countries. Few people live in the forest areas, and some species of animals, especially large mammals such as wolves and bears, have survived here when they have become extinct in much of the rest of Europe. The Canary Islands are also known worldwide for their wildlife, and four of Spain's 14 national parks can be found there.

▲ *Bears are being reintroduced to the Pyrenees from forests in Eastern Europe as part of a joint venture between Spain and France.*

IT'S A FACT!

After the last breeding female bear in the Pyrenees was killed by a French hunter in 2004, the French and Spanish governments developed a program for bringing more bears from Slovenia in Eastern Europe to be released into the mountains. Today, the bear population is on the rise.

Spain's Threatened Landscape

As in many countries, some of Spain's natural environments are under threat. Forests have been destroyed by fires, but others are being cut down to make way for building developments as the country's population increases and more space is needed for human settlement. Global climate change threatens much of the Meseta with desertification. Spain receives a lot of rainfall, but there are still water shortages, as more and more water from the rivers is used for irrigating farmland. Wetland areas are also shrinking as water is diverted from rivers, which is threatening the wildlife that make the wetlands their home.

IT'S A FACT!

Spain is a very important location for bird migration between Africa and Europe because it is one of only three routes across the Mediterranean. The others are Libya to the toe of Italy and the coastal regions of the eastern Mediterranean.

▼ *The wetlands around Spanish deltas— where rivers enter the sea—are important habitats for wildlife, but water shortages are now threatening these areas.*

▲ *Spain is a world leader in solar power. Solar farms use huge panels like these to capture the energy from sunlight and turn it into electricity.*

A Sustainable Future

Spain is a world leader in using renewable energy sources—such as the sun, wind, and water—to generate electricity. Spain's thousands of rivers are used to generate hydroelectricity as well as for irrigation. Spain is also the world's second biggest producer of electricity from wind power, after Germany, but because Spain has only half the population of Germany, this makes its environmental record more impressive. The Navarre region of Spain has a program that intends to supply 100 percent of its energy needs from renewable resources by 2010.

GLOBAL LEADER

Solar Power

In 2008, the largest solar farm in the world opened in southeast Spain. The Jumilla farm is made up of 120,000 solar panels that convert sunlight into electricity, which can power 20,000 homes. Using renewable resources like the sun helps preserve supplies of fossil fuels, which are running out, and reduces the amount of carbon dioxide being released into the atmosphere.

Population and Migration

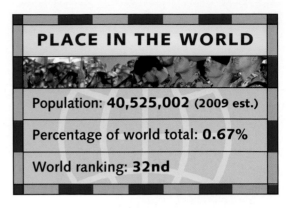

The people who live in Spain's different regions have their own cultures and traditions, but Spain has also become a multicultural society thanks to the large number of immigrants who have settled there, particularly in the last 20 years.

PLACE IN THE WORLD

Population: **40,525,002** (2009 est.)

Percentage of world total: **0.67%**

World ranking: **32nd**

Migration to the Cities

In the middle of the nineteenth century, people began moving from the countryside in the west and south of Spain, to developing cities in the northeast in places such as Catalonia and the Basque Country. They hoped to find better job opportunities there and to improve their quality of life. This resulted in the spread of traditions from one part of the country to another, as the migrants kept their own cultures alive by celebrating traditional customs and fiestas.

▶ *This "whale parade" is part of the traditional Semana Grande fiesta in the Basque Country.*

Fleeing Abroad

During and after the Spanish Civil War (1936), many refugees from the Basque Country and Catalonia crossed the Pyrenees to France, because they were afraid of staying in Spain while it was ruled by Francisco Franco. Refugees from Galicia and Asturias in the northwest emigrated across the Atlantic Ocean and settled in the United States. Later, even more Spanish people from all regions moved to wealthy countries, especially Germany, in search of better prospects. Emigration caused problems for Spain in the second half of the twentieth century. The economy declined because so many people moved abroad. This especially affected rural areas, where there were not enough young people to work on the farms or enough children to keep schools open.

Immigration

During the 1970s, Spain's fortunes began to rise, and when Franco died many migrants returned home. In 1986, Spain joined the European Union (EU). This meant that its links with other European countries were strengthened, and the economy began to improve. People from other countries started moving to Spain and immigrants now make up about 10 percent of the population—far more than in any other EU country. Spain's long history of migration and emigration means that most Spaniards today are very understanding of the difficulties immigrants face, and are tolerant of them in their country.

◀ Locutorios sometimes sell particular products, such as halal meat (prepared in a special way), to the Muslim community. The word carniceria means "butchers."

IT STARTED HERE

Locutorios

Locutorios are special shops that provide Internet access and phones with low fees for immigrants to call home. Many *Locutorios* sell special products, such as exotic fruits, and they are often the center of a local community.

Immigrant Origins

Most immigrants in Spain come from former colonies in Latin America. They have the advantage of speaking Spanish, but many of them—especially women—do not have any qualifications and work in low-paid jobs in the tourism industry, or as domestic helpers. The second largest group comes from countries in northwest Africa, especially Morocco. Few of these immigrants speak Spanish when they arrive, and many work as unskilled laborers in the construction industry and in farming.

Eastern European Immigrants

The third largest group comes from Eastern Europe. These immigrants have helped meet Spain's need for skilled workers, especially in industries like construction. However, as the economies of countries in Eastern Europe improve, many of these workers will return home.

GOING GLOBAL

Immigration has had a big impact on the pop-music culture in Spain. Top bands such as Ojos de Brujo (which means "Wizard's Eyes") fuse Flamenco themes with other world music to create their own unique style, called "jipjop flamenkillo." The band has become popular in other countries, and was awarded a BBC World Music Award in 2004.

▶ *Spain has a booming construction industry, which attracts workers from many other countries. These workers are from Chile in South America.*

Future Challenges

Spain has had to meet the needs of its fast-growing population, and services such as schools and health care have to be paid for. As immigrants often work in low-paid or temporary employment, this can cause problems in regions that have weak economies. Because so many Spanish people have personal experience of being migrants, they do not mind the numbers of immigrants in their country. This could change, however, if numbers increase and fewer jobs are available.

▲ *Although many Spanish people are tolerant of immigrants, some groups do not like the numbers of foreigners settling in their country. These people are part of a fascist group protesting against immigration.*

Culture and Lifestyles

Spanish culture is celebrated in everyday life, not just on holidays or special occasions. There are not only famous national fiestas, such as Semana Santa (Easter week), but also each region—even every village—has its own unique Fiesta Mayor in charge of the activities.

¡Fiesta!

Dozens of different events take place during the Spanish fiestas: big events such as bulls running through the streets of Pamplona, or Valencia's Las Fallas, where huge statues—which take months to prepare—are lit up. Some events occur only in certain regions. In Catalonia, for example, *Els Castellers* make human towers or "castles" up to 11 stories high. Smaller towns and villages offer their own versions of traditional favorites like giants, dwarfs, dancing devils, or fire-breathing dragons.

A Communal Effort

All these spectacular traditions are the work of local groups, often based in communities within large cities. Some groups are small, almost family affairs, but others are huge, with hundreds of members. Many people return to their home town or village to help celebrate the fiesta, even if they moved away years ago.

▶ *Children as young as six years old train hard to reach the top of the amazing Casteller towers.*

▲ *Bull-running is a traditional event at many Spanish fiestas. People clear the way as these fearsome animals charge down the streets.*

Catholic Traditions

All fiestas are centered around a serious religious celebration, usually to honor the local patron saint. Catholicism was the only religion allowed in Spain from the time the Moors left until the nineteenth century. Francisco Franco made it very difficult for non-Catholics in Spain. For example, people had to be Catholic to be allowed to work as civil servants. Since Franco's time, some Spaniards have switched to follow other Christian faiths. Large numbers of Muslims have arrived from African countries, and mosques have opened all over Spain.

FAMOUS SPANIARD

Penelope Cruz (b. 1974)

Spain's leading film stars such as Penelope Cruz have broken language barriers to become famous in the "capital" of the movie world, Hollywood. Cruz was born in Madrid and began acting on television. In 2009, she was the first Spanish actress to win an Academy Award, for the film *Vicky Cristina Barcelona*.

Sport Crazy!

Soccer, called *futbol* in Spanish, is the most popular sport in Spain. Leading clubs, such as Real Madrid, attract top players from around the world, and rival club FC Barcelona proved it was the best team in Europe by winning the European Cup in 2009. Basketball, a sport "imported" from the United States, has become extremely popular in Spain. The Spanish basketball team reached the final in the 2008 Beijing Olympic Games.

▼ *Spain takes on the United States in the basketball final of the 2008 Olympic Games in Beijing, China.*

FAMOUS SPANIARD

Rafael Nadal (b. 1986)

Spaniard Rafael Nadal—or Rafa, as he is known in Spain—was the world's best tennis player in 2008. He was born in Majorca and started playing tennis when he was three years old. He was ranked No. 1 in the world after winning nearly every major tournament in the 2008 season.

Popular Music

Young people in Spain have been greatly influenced by aspects of popular culture from around the world. Pop groups from the United States and Britain are very popular with young Spaniards. A number of Spanish musicians and singers have also found worldwide fame, including Enrique Iglesias, who has sold over 60 million albums around the world.

Keeping Customs

Although there is a Spanish film industry, many young people enjoy American films. Some older people worry that traditional Spanish culture will be lost as young people are more exposed to the culture of English-speaking countries such as the United States and the United Kingdom. However, the popularity of traditions such as fiestas keep local customs and languages alive.

Youth Culture

Children and young people are always included in all aspects of Spanish life, whether it is sports, fiestas, religion, or family affairs such as Sunday lunch. They are usually allowed to stay up later than children in the United States and the United Kingdom. Spanish youngsters are extremely independent and go out on their own from their early teens. This independence often starts as young as six or seven years old, when they may attend summer camps and join children's sections of sports clubs and fiesta groups.

▲ *Groups like Calima draw music from all over the world and fuse it with Flamenco.*

THE HOME OF...

La Siesta

Part of the Spanish lifestyle is to take a mid-afternoon nap, called a *siesta*. In some places, shops close while people rest, and then open again later. The *siesta* makes possible the round-the-clock lifestyle that is a big feature of Spanish life.

Economy and Trade

Membership in the European Union has allowed Spain to sell its products to other countries, and has encouraged foreign companies to invest, creating jobs and generating wealth. However, like many countries, Spain has suffered in the recent global economic crisis.

Agriculture

Because Spain is situated in the sunny south of Europe, it is ideally suited for agriculture. Traditional crops such as olives and grapes grow well in the Spanish climate, so Spain can make olive oil and wine to sell abroad. Recently, thanks to technology such as irrigation and refrigerated transport, fruit and vegetables also grow in abundance and fetch high prices around the world, particularly in Northern Europe.

▼ *Spain's climate makes it ideal for growing crops such as grapes, and vineyards like this in Seville can be seen in many parts of the country.*

GLOBAL LEADER

Olive Oil

Spain is the world's biggest producer of olive oil—generating 36 percent of global production and exporting much of this to other countries. Spaniards consume nearly 30 lbs. (14 kg) of olive oil each per year. It is often used instead of butter or margarine in sandwiches.

Industry

By the 1970s, traditional Spanish industries, such as shipbuilding, were facing competition from countries in the Far East, whose prices were much cheaper. To improve its own industry, Spain encouraged investment from foreign companies. Now it is a leading manufacturer of cars and electrical appliances. Although many of these products are made in Spain, the companies that make them are owned by other countries.

Natural Resources

Spain does not have a lot of natural resources. Most of its coal and iron have already been used up, so Spain has to import these materials. However, Spanish companies have been involved in finding and extracting oil and gas throughout the world. This not only supplies Spain with fuel, but also means that Spanish companies bring profits back to Spain.

▲ *Spain's important car industry is largely owned by foreign companies. There is a risk that jobs may be lost as owners move factories abroad.*

Real Estate

Building and construction are an important part of the Spanish economy. In 2007, Spain built around 800,000 new houses—more than France, Germany, and the United Kingdom put together. This does not include all the hotels, hospitals, shopping malls, roads, and railways that are also being built.

Services

Among Spain's most important service industries are finance and telecommunications. Spain is an important "bridge" between the economies of Europe and Latin America, because Spanish banks share a common language and similar legal system. Spanish companies have also developed new technologies in these areas that can rival that of countries such as the United States.

▲ *Most building projects, especially homes, are paid for by loans or mortgages, and during the boom period families as well as companies became very much in debt.*

GOING GLOBAL

Banco Santander is the largest bank in the Eurozone—the countries that have adopted the euro as their currency. It is part of the Santander group, Spain's largest banking corporation, which leads the banking sector in the Spanish-speaking world. As countries all over the world experienced an economic crisis in the late 2000s, the Santander group took over several big banks in countries including the UK.

Tourism

Tourism is an important industry in Spain. World-famous sites such as Madrid's El Prado art gallery or the architecture in Barcelona attract hundreds of thousands of tourist visitors from all over the world. However, most people visit Spain to enjoy beach holidays in the hot coastal resorts. Millions of people from Northern Europe flock to Spain's Mediterranean coast to enjoy the guaranteed sunshine and relaxed lifestyle. The Spanish are enthusiastic tourists, too, and travel the world seeking new cultures and experiences.

IT STARTED HERE

Package Vacations

Mass tourism in the sun took off in Spain after the invention of the package vacation in the 1950s. After spending many family vacations in Spain, thousands of people from Northern Europe decide to live in Spain when they retire.

▼ *Thousands of tourists visit Barcelona every year to look at the famous architecture. Much of it—like these "gingerbread houses"—was designed by architect Antoni Gaudí.*

Government and Politics

When Francisco Franco died, Spain shifted from being a dictatorship to a democracy. It adopted a new constitution, which has been very successful. Spain now has a respected role in world affairs, helped by its membership in international organizations such as the European Union, the United Nations, and NATO.

The Cortez

Franco named King Juan Carlos as his "heir," hoping that he would continue to rule as dictator. However, Juan Carlos actually encouraged the move toward democracy, and the new constitution was adopted in 1978. Today, the Spanish parliament—called the Cortez—has two chambers: the Senate, which passes new laws, and the Congress of Deputies, which makes decisions about running the country. Many responsibilities, such as health care and education, are left to local governments called autonomous regions.

▼ *The* Congreso de los Diputados *(Congress of Deputies) in the Spanish parliament.*

The Role of Autonomous Regions

Some autonomous regions have more powers than others, and it can be difficult to achieve a balance between those who want more political freedom, or even full independence, and others who want Spain to be a more united country under a single government. The Basque Country and Catalonia are the most industrialized and highly populated regions in Spain, and they attract migrants from the rest of the country as well as immigrants from abroad. The political influence of the regions is important to the Cortez, as most governments depend on cooperation between local branches of the two main political parties.

IT'S A FACT!

There are 17 autonomous regions in Spain. Each one manages public services like health care and education. The regions have their own parliament and hold their own elections, as well as send representatives to the Cortez.

▼ *Within each region there are city, or municipal, councils led by a city mayor. These buildings in Seville house the local government offices.*

The Threat of Terrorism

Catalonia and the Basque Country once owned land across the Pyrenees in France. In the case of the Basque Country, a terrorist group called ETA has used these links to hide from the police. Members of ETA want the Basque Country to be an independent state and they use terrorist methods to fight for this cause. The Spanish authorities work closely with their French counterparts to combat this threat.

International Relations

Spain's move to democracy was marked when it joined two important international organizations—NATO in 1982 and the European Union in 1986. Some people feel that allowing the European government more control over issues, such as those concerning the environment, could solve some political problems over autonomy and independence. For this reason, Spaniards are eager to support the development of the EU.

▲ *ETA terrorists being arrested over the border in France. ETA violence still poses a threat to Spain's stability, but membership in the EU may change these issues.*

An Atlantic Rift?

NATO is a military alliance between countries in Western Europe and the United States. However, General Franco allowed Americans to build military bases in Spain long before it became a member of NATO, and many Spaniards feel that the United States helped Franco stay in power. Although Spain sends troops and money to NATO missions in war zones such as Afghanistan and Kosovo, it is often suspicious of American motives. In 2004, Spain withdrew its troops from the war in Iraq, as the prime minister felt that the U.S.-led invasion was unjustified.

▲ *Crown Prince Felipe of Spain inspects Spanish troops in Afghanistan in 2008. The troops were sent there as a peacekeeping force and to help with reconstruction.*

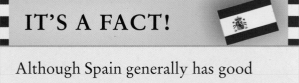

IT'S A FACT!

Although Spain generally has good international relationships, there are currently border disputes with Morocco (Ceuta and Melilla), Portugal (Olivenza), and the UK (Gibraltar).

Spain in 2020

It is likely that Spain's influence in the world will continue to grow as its population increases and its economy improves. Many current issues will need to be dealt with, though, including the wealth divide between people in the north and south, and the demands by some Basque people for complete independence.

Regional Differences

In a changing world, the Spanish people will need to unite to react to global influences such as competition for jobs and investment. However, the influence of regional governments in national affairs may make this difficult. For example, at the moment, the Catalan government is trying to gain more economic independence, and in doing so it is putting its own needs before the needs of the country as a whole. Many of the factories that were built during Spain's boom years from the mid-1960s onward are now closing in the face of competition from Eastern Europe. Catalonia's more advanced economy may be able to meet this challenge, but other parts of Spain may not be able to compete.

◀ Infrastructure projects, including high-speed trains and rail links—such as this subway in Seville—need to take the whole country into account, not just the individual regions.

New Influences

By 2020, the governments of all the regions of Spain are likely to reflect the different ethnic groups in a way they do not currently. This may change the way Spain views itself and its place in the world. Even though immigration is thought to be decreasing, and some groups such as people from Eastern Europe are likely to return home as their prospects improve, the changes in society will be permanent. By 2020, a large proportion of people born in Spain will have many different ethnic origins, and all children will be raised in a country that is influenced more by the outside world than by its internal geography and history.

▶ *Festivals such as the Semana Grande celebrate the individual traditions of the Spanish regions. In the future, this pride in their unique heritage may lead some regions to demand complete independence from Spain.*

Glossary

autonomous having a certain amount of political freedom. Spain's autonomous regions have some self-government, and control matters such as health care and education.

colony a country or a region that is under the political control of another country.

constitution a set of rules for a country, outlining the basic principles of its government.

democracy a political system in which the people of a country choose their leaders through elections.

desertification the process in which land that was once used for farming or other human activities turns into a desert.

dictator someone who has complete control over a country and its people.

economy the financial system of a country or region, including how much money is made from the production and sale of goods and services.

Eurozone the name given to the group of 16 countries that use the euro as their unit of currency.

export to transport products or materials abroad for sale or trade.

Fascist a method of government in which the ruler takes away the rights of the citizens and rules the country as a dictator.

fossil fuels resources from the Earth, such as coal, oil, and natural gas, that come from the remains of ancient plants and animals.

hydroelectricity electricity that is generated using the energy from running water.

immigrant a person who has moved to another country to live.

import to bring in goods or materials from another country for sale.

Industrial Revolution a period in the eighteenth and nineteenth centuries when machines were invented that could do work once carried out by people.

Latin America the parts of Central and South America where the Romance languages, originating from Latin, are spoken.

refugee someone who has had to flee from their own country because of war or persecution.

renewable resources resources that can be used for energy to make electricity that will not run out, such as wind, water, and the sun.

terrorists people who use violence or cause fear to try and change a political system or policy.

wetland an area of marshy land.

Further Information

Books

Focus on Spain
World in Focus
by Polly Campbell, Simon Rice, and
Rob Bowden
(World Almanac Library, 2007)

Latin America
by Louise I. Gerdes
(Greenhaven Press, 2009)

Spain
Living In…
by Su Kent
(Sea to Sea Publications, 2007)

Spain
Nations of the World
by Nathaniel Harris
(Raintree, 2004)

Spain
QEB Travel Through
by John Kenyon
(QEB Publishing, 2008)

The Transcontinental Treaty, 1819
by Meg Greene
(Rosen Central Primary
Source, 2009)

Web Sites

http://www.spain-info.com
A site with plenty of information on the country,
including history, maps, and more.

http://www.socialstudiesforkids.com/subjects/
economics.htm
Get to grips with economics with this site where topics
such as money, trade, and budgets are explained.

http://www.travelforkids.com/Funtodo/Spain/
spain.htm
Take a journey through Spain with this fun site.

https://www.cia.gov/library/publications/the-world-
factbook/geos/sp.html
The CIA World Factbook with information on Spain.

*Every effort has been made by the publisher to ensure
that these web sites contain no inappropriate or offensive
material. However, because of the nature of the Internet,
it is impossible to guarantee that the contents of these sites
will not be altered. We strongly advise that Internet access
is supervised by a responsible adult.*

Index

Numbers in **bold** indicate pictures.